D0948955

Viking

LONDON, NEW YORK,
MELBOURNE, MUNICH, and DELHI

Written and edited by Carrie Love
and Lorrie Mack
Designed by Penny Lamprell,
Sadie Thomas, Tory Gordon-Harris,
and Clare Shedden
Publishing manager Susan Leonard
Managing art editor Rachael Foster
Picture researcher Liz Moore
Production Sarah Jenkins
DTP designer Ben Hung
Illustrator Andy Cooke
Jacket designer Mary Sandberg
Jacket editor Mariza O'Keeffe
Consultant Angus Konstam
US editor Margaret Parrish

Thank you to Murton Park, York, UK,
for allowing us to take photos of their
reconstruction of a Viking village.

First American Edition, 2007
Published in the United States by
DK Publishing, Inc., 375 Hudson Street
New York, New York 10014

07 08 09 10 10 9 8 7 6 5 4 3 2 1
ED507—05/07

ISBN 978-0-75662-906-9 (hardcover)
ISBN 978-0-75662-907-6 (ALB)

Color reproduction by Colorscan, Singapore
Printed and bound in Italy by L.E.G.O.
Discover more at
www.dk.com

Contents

Wherever the Vikings lived, experts have built
reconstructions of their homes and farms, and people
dress up as Vikings to re-create their way of life.
To bring the Viking world alive, we have used
pictures of these reconstructions in this book.

Meet the Vikings

Over a thousand years ago, from the 8th to the 11th centuries, the Vikings set out to explore and raid countries across the world. Vikings came from Scandinavia—Norway, Sweden, and Denmark.

Mystery man

The Vikings didn't paint or draw, but they were great carvers and modelers. This small silver head may be a god, a hero, or a warrior.

GREENLAND

ICELAND

ATLANTIC OCEAN

NORTH AMERICA

Follow the arrows and take an ocean voyage with the Vikings.

Exploring the world

In their fine ships, the Vikings explored, raided, and traded across Europe, Russia, and the Middle East. They even got as far as Iceland, Greenland, and North America.

LABRADOR

NEWFOUNDLAND

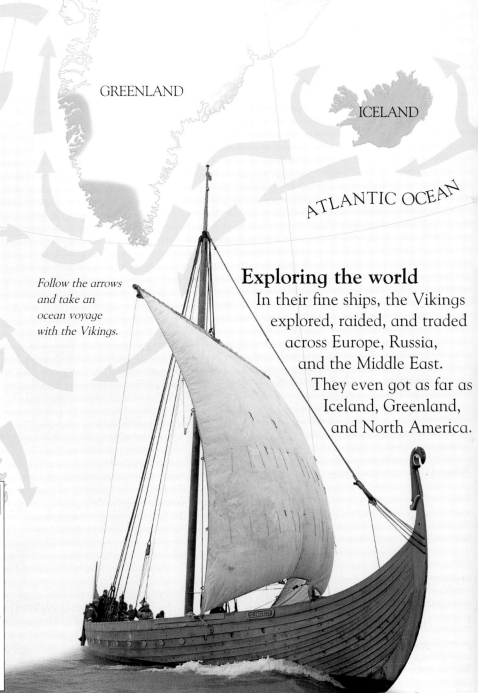

Viking words

Viking: from *vikingr*, an old Norwegian word for "sea raider."

Thing: local assembly, where people could exchange ideas.

Karl, jarl, thrall: Free person, noble person, slave.

Skald: Composer of poems about kings and heroes.

4

This map
shows the
routes many
Vikings
may have
travelled.

Homelands

Settlements

Masters of craft

Vikings were not just excellent sailors and
fighters—they were skilled craftspeople
who made beautiful jewelry, textiles,
metalwork, and furniture.

RUSSIA

FINLAND

*Elaborate
oval brooch
worked in gold.*

NORWAY

SWEDEN

DENMARK

NORTH
SEA

*Helmets
were made
from iron
plates welded
together.*

*Skilled
blacksmiths
made strong,
sharp swords.*

EUROPE

BRITISH
ISLES

FRANCE

Mighty warriors

Fast and fierce
in attack, Viking
warriors were feared
everywhere. With
strength and speed
on their side, they
launched violent
raids on rich
towns, farms,
and monasteries.

Ruling the sea

The Vikings were skilled sailors. Their well-built warships and longships carried them on dangerous voyages through rough seas, hidden rocks, and jagged icebergs.

Artist's impression of a Viking warship with a mythical beast as a figurehead.

Versatile vessels

Viking longships—the longest and fastest Viking warships—were special as they could be rowed or sailed. Vikings used the oars to row through rivers and coastal waters. The large sail helped them get through open waters.

ARE WE THERE YET?

The Vikings had no form of compass so they navigated by staying close to land when they could, or by using the Sun and stars to work out their position. The Vikings learned from experience and passed on information from one generation to the next. They had a good knowledge of fish, seabirds, wind, and wave patterns that helped them to steer in the right direction and survive at sea.

Superb ships

Vikings made a range of ships and boats for various purposes. There were warships (usually longships), ferries (which carried passengers across rivers and fjords), small rowing boats (used on lakes), cargo ships, and fishing boats.

This prow ends with a snake's head in a spiral.

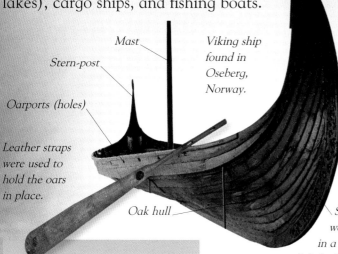

Mast

Stern-post

Viking ship found in Oseberg, Norway.

Oarports (holes)

Leather straps were used to hold the oars in place.

Oak hull

Intricate carvings of animals

Strakes (planks) of wood were overlapped in a technique called "clinker" boatbuilding.

Valued heritage

Viking carving plays an important role in Scandinavian culture and tourism. This prow adorns a modern sightseeing ship in Stockholm.

Vikings frightened their enemies with ferocious figureheads.

Viking ships were adaptable and fast. They were also easy to navigate through narrow and shallow rivers.

Scary heads

The Vikings often carved figureheads of beasts and dragons on their ship prows to scare off their enemies. Some wooden figureheads may have been detachable so that the Vikings could position them before they landed.

Daring discoveries

Using their superb skills as shipbuilders and navigators, the Vikings set off across the ocean to find new lands to colonize and farm. The Vikings landed in North America, centuries before Christopher Columbus. They also discovered Iceland and Greenland.

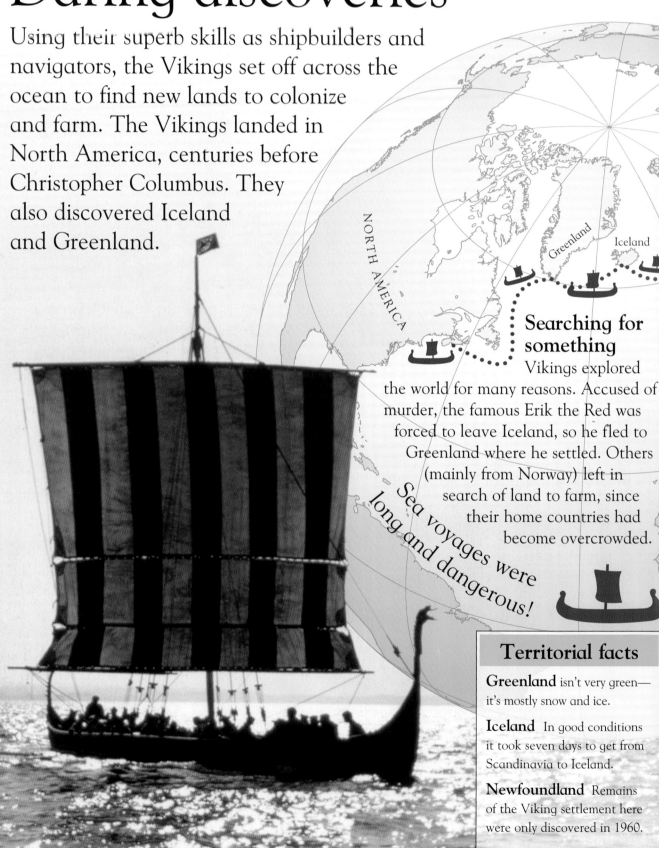

Searching for something

Vikings explored the world for many reasons. Accused of murder, the famous Erik the Red was forced to leave Iceland, so he fled to Greenland where he settled. Others (mainly from Norway) left in search of land to farm, since their home countries had become overcrowded.

Sea voyages were long and dangerous!

Territorial facts

Greenland isn't very green—it's mostly snow and ice.

Iceland In good conditions it took seven days to get from Scandinavia to Iceland.

Newfoundland Remains of the Viking settlement here were only discovered in 1960.

Land of ice

The Vikings discovered Iceland in 870 CE. The inner area of the land is hard to inhabit, with its mountains, glaciers, and active volcanoes. Settlements were built around the coast because it was green and fertile—by 930 CE many people lived there.

This was the site where the Althing (see page 31) met in Iceland.

What's in a name?

By choosing Greenland as the name for the snowy country he explored, Erik the Red encouraged people to move there. As a result, Vikings established two large settlements in areas that were good for farming. They raised sheep and cattle, but relied on seals and reindeer for food.

Statue in Iceland of Leif the Lucky (see below), who was Erik the Red's son.

Viking ruins in Greenland

Reconstruction of a Viking settlement in L'Anse aux Meadows, Newfoundland (modern Canada).

A new world

Leif the Lucky was the first European to set foot in North America. His Viking colony in Newfoundland is not just the oldest European settlement in the New World—it's the only one.

9

The Viking terror

Traveling Vikings not only discovered new territories, they also invaded towns, cities, and smaller settlements throughout Europe. They attacked from the sea or sailed up rivers in search of treasure they could carry off. Sometimes, they even demanded huge payments to leave.

Fourteenth-century manuscript showing the Viking invasion of Britain several centuries earlier.

Warriors attacking from the sea could raid, loot, and sail away before the local ruler could arrive to protect his townspeople.

Smash and grab
Bands of Vikings usually arrived by ship to attack farms, churches, and monasteries by surprise. They then plundered them for valuables, money, and slaves.

Viking marauders were carved on this gravestone at Lindisfarne monastery.

Holy ruins

The monastery on the holy island of Lindisfarne (off northeast England) was raided repeatedly by Vikings who, in 793 CE, slaughtered the monks and stole their treasures. Today, only its ruins remain.

Paris under siege

This Victorian illustration brings to life a violent Viking attack on Paris in 865 CE, led by a chieftain called Rollo.

Viking longships were built to navigate shallow waters and land on flat shorelines.

This bishop's cross from Ireland was taken to Sweden by Vikings.

These coins date from the period of Viking rule in Ireland.

Victory in Ireland

The Vikings began to raid Ireland in 795 CE, and by the 820s they had worked their way around the coast and moved inland. Dublin became first a base from which to attack the rest of the country, then a busy Viking center for trade with other lands.

Attack facts

● Some Vikings who raided northern France settled there. The area became known as Normandy—"land of north men."

● One Viking band took 62 ships to Spain, Italy, and Africa.

● The Vikings first began to raid at the end of the eighth century.

Weapons and warriors

Vikings were daring and courageous in war, following their lord or king into any conflict. Warriors believed that honor and glory in battle lasted forever, even beyond death. Their most prized possessions—their weapons—were often buried with them.

Warrior god

In this engraving Tyr, Viking god of heroic combat, wears a bear's head as a helmet and a bearskin cloak.

Viking swords were double-edged—both edges of the blade were sharpened.

Symbols of power

Great leaders carried weapons with precious and intricate decoration that showed their importance. This iron ax head is inlaid with silver wire.

Broad ax blade

The end of a sword is called a pommel.

Spearhead

Viking shields were round and made of wood, like this replica used in reenactments.

Men of iron

Viking weapons were made of iron, sometimes decorated with copper or silver. To make sharp steel edges, carbon was added to the iron when it was hot.

Horse power

While early warriors fought on foot, later Vikings were skilled horsemen. This silver figure dates from the 10th century.

Battlegrounds

Viking warfare was brutal and bloody. Warriors saw battle as a noble pursuit, and those who proved themselves were often rewarded with land and riches.

HORNS NOT REQUIRED

We think of Viking warriors as wearing scary horned helmets, but there's little evidence to support this image—few examples survive, and experts think these were used for religious rituals. During the 1800s, Romantic artists first portrayed Vikings with horns, and it's their pictures that keep the myth alive.

VIKING AUDITION

No horns!

Vikings usually won their battles by surprise attack. In new lands, they would arrive by boat, strike on foot, then return to their ship.

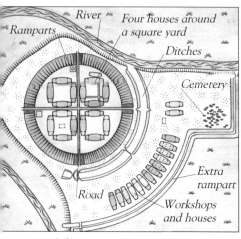

The layout diagram labels: River, Four houses around a square yard, Ramparts, Ditches, Cemetery, Extra rampart, Road, Workshops and houses

Living in a fort

Around 980 CE, the Vikings built four large circular forts (Aggersborg, Fyrkat, Trelleborg, and Nonebakken) in Denmark. Historians think King Harald Bluetooth ordered their construction to show his rule and symbolize his power.

Adding on

Trelleborg differed slightly from the other forts—it had 15 houses outside the main ramparts, protected by an extra rampart.

The layout of a Viking fort was geometric, and circular ramparts made of soil, turf, and wood kept enemies out.

Trelleborg (shown above) was 445 ft (136 m) wide.

Building the past

At Fyrkat fort, a Viking house has been carefully re-created. Its main door leads into a small entrance area. This opens onto a huge central living space.

The mighty sword

At Trelleborg, people reenact scenes from Viking life. Here, warriors use swords for fierce hand-to-hand combat. Real Vikings gave their weapons names like "leg-biter" or "killer." Those who were wealthy had their swords decorated on the hilt (handle).

Viking shields were made from wood with metal or leather rims.

The tiny notch in this arrowhead is designed to cut feathers for the ends of arrows.

Smiths are craftsmen who work with metal. This smith is hammering sharp heads for the tips of arrows.

Hard at work

At Fyrkat fort, two longhouses were used as "smithies"—workshops where smiths made weapons and jewelry from iron, silver, and gold.

Viking forts also had carpentry workshops.

Smiths made Viking spears, which had long, sharp blades.

The most popular Viking weapons were axes with long wooden handles.

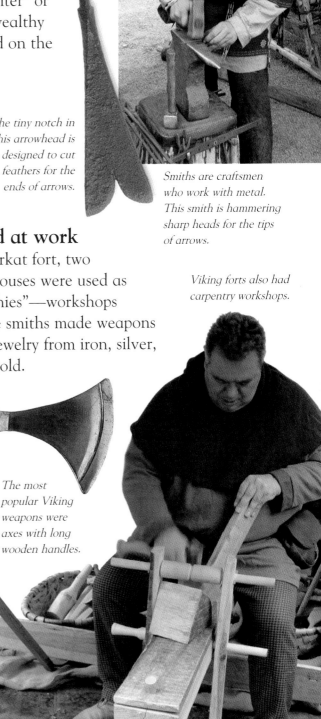

Home life

Viking houses were usually rectangular and large enough to house more than one generation of a family. Poor people had few possessions and little luxury, but wealthy homes might feature wooden furniture and decorative wall panels.

Practical solutions

Building materials varied around the Viking world. Turf (above), bark, or thatch (below) were used for the roof if lumber was unavailable.

Thatch is made from straw.

Domestic facts

- Women were in charge of the family's valuables.

- In most homes, everyone slept in the same room. Rich people, though, had a separate room from their servants.

- Houses were lit with torches made from bundles of straw.

Wild walls

Some Viking houses had a traditional wattle-and-daub construction. The woven branches that form the basic structure are called wattle.

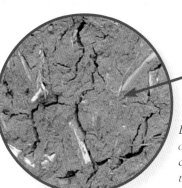

Daub, a mixture of clay and dung, coated the wattle to seal it.

The basic plan

Most Viking houses had a single central living room. People sat and slept on raised platforms lining the walls. This reconstruction is partly finished— the wattle is in place, but not the daub.

Lock it up

Vikings didn't have much furniture, but they kept their valuables in locked chests. Keys were symbols of responsibility.

Ninth-century bronze key found in Denmark

The hearth of the home

Vikings ate, drank, and socialized around a raised stone hearth on the stamped dirt floor. The fire was needed for warmth, for cooking, and for light.

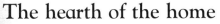

Men wore either round or peaked hats. Some peaked hats had silver ornaments at the top.

Getting dressed

For every day, Vikings wore clothes made from plain wool. Tunics and dresses may have had woven, colored borders. The very rich wore clothes decorated with gold and silver thread.

Most Viking brooches were oval in shape.

Perfect miniatures

Viking children looked like small versions of their parents. Boys wore tunics over pants and girls wore dresses and aprons.

Vikings kept their hair tidy with combs that were very much like ours, except they were carved from bone.

An eye for fashion

Viking women wore long underdresses with aprons on top. Men wore long, tuniclike shirts over woolen pants, often with a cloak. Both men and women used brooches; women had two to fasten their aprons, and men had one to fasten their cloaks.

Both poor and rich wore leather shoes, usually made of goatskin.

The well-dressed warrior

Wealthy warriors wore heavy leather or chain-mail tunics and metal helmets. Their cloaks were arranged to keep the fighting arm free. The strap that carried their sword was called a baldric.

Chain mail was very heavy, but flexible.

This iron helmet has a noseguard and a band of chain mail at the back to protect the warrior's neck.

Chain mail is woven from thousands of iron links, each one forged separately.

High-ranking warriors wore wolfskin.

Leather belt with bronze buckle

Fighting from the ranks

When they went to war for their local noble or chieftain, peasants had no protective clothing. They carried a weapon—an ax or a spear— and a wooden shield.

Peasants were freemen, not slaves. Most were farmers.

Ax

Shield

Viking warriors were unlike modern soldiers: they didn't have a uniform. Every man had to provide his own clothes and weapons.

Viking jewelry

Viking men and women loved jewelry—they wore rings, brooches, bracelets, and necklaces. The poor made their jewelry from bronze, pewter, or bone, whereas the rich used silver and gold.

Images from mythology often decorate Viking jewelry. This etched pendant takes its shape from Thor's hammer.

Followers of fashion

Vikings tended to adapt designs from other countries. This huge dress pin (which was more for display than practicality) was based on a style the Vikings saw in the British Isles.

Silver pin and ring inlaid with gold

Vikings used the black compound niello (made from silver, copper, and lead) for engraving.

Shining symbols

- Vikings displayed their status with the jewelry they wore.

- Kings rewarded successful raiders with precious jewelry.

- Valuables were buried underground in hoards. The largest ever found contained 90 lb (40 kg) of silver.

This intricate brooch was made from sheet gold pressed into a lead die.

Practical purposes

Vikings didn't have buttons or zippers—everything that couldn't be tied or belted was fastened with a pin or a brooch.

Hoop and heart detailing were added using twisted gold wire and filled in with extra blobs of the precious metal.

Around their necks

Gold, silver, amber, and glass were used for Viking bead necklaces. Pendants may have been worn on chains or strips of leather. Viking neck rings were sometimes made by melting down silver Arab coins.

Considered valuable, beads were gathered up during raids. Vikings could also buy beads in their own markets.

Necklace made of glass beads

Craftsmen melted down broken glass to make bright beads.

This necklace is made of boar tusks, amber, and glass beads. Animal bones left over from cooking were often used to make jewelry.

Rings everywhere

Only Swedish women wore earrings, but male and female Vikings from all over wore rings on their fingers, arms, and neck. Gold, jet, colored glass, and amber were all used to make finger rings.

Men and women both wore finger rings.

The fine decoration on this gold arm ring was applied with a stamp.

21

Living off the land

Although their land was often barren and overcrowded, Vikings relied on farming for their food. As a result, some people moved to faraway lands in search of fertile soil and bigger farms for their crops and animals.

Vikings made grain into flour by placing it between the two halves of a quern stone, then turning a wooden handle to grind the top against the bottom.

Top
Bottom

Jarlshof farm

When it was built, this ruined 9th-century Viking farmhouse in Scotland had two rooms—a main hall and a kitchen. The farmer and his family would have slept on platforms against the wall.

Table crops

In addition to gathering wild vegetables, Vikings grew them on the land. They at vegetables that grew well in cool climates, such as carrots, parsnips, turnips, wild celery, leeks, onions, peas, and cabbages.

Useful beasts

Vikings raised cattle for their meat and their hide, but mostly for their milk, which was used to make butter and cheese.

Useful tool

Vikings cut cloth, sheared sheep, and trimmed their beards with shears like these.

Vikings made clothes and bedding from sheep's wool.

25

Making meals

To cook their food and warm their houses, Vikings kept fires burning all day, which made their homes very smoky. Families ate their main meal in the evening, after sunset.

Fish was dried to preserve it through the winter.

Fishy facts
People in coastal areas depended on seafood for much of their diet. Those who lived inland ate freshwater fish.

On the fire
Food was cooked in cauldrons over an open fire. These pots, made from iron or soapstone, were suspended from a hook on a three-legged stand, or tripod.

Pots of clay
Early Vikings mostly used wooden containers for food but later on, clay pots were common. The holes in this round pot show where a patch was once stuck over the crack.

Varied diet

In addition to fish and meat, Vikings ate eggs, vegetables, and fruit such as berries. They used herbs to season soups and stews.

Daily bread

Most Vikings ate bread made from barley rather than wheat flour; it was baked over a fire on a griddle. Rich people ate wheat-flour bread that was baked in an oven.

Game birds such as duck were caught in traps or hunted with short arrows.

Fair game

In addition to hares, Vikings trapped and hunted deer, bears, elk, wild boars, reindeer, whales, and seals for food.

Food words

Cauldron: a huge pot for cooking food over a fire.

Griddle: a flat metal plate used as a cooking surface.

Preserve: to stop food from going bad.

Season: to flavor food with herbs and spices.

Super skills

The incredible success of the Viking race was largely due to their craft skills. They made strong, fast ships, sharp weapons, beautiful jewelry, durable clothes, and sturdy wooden tools and household items.

Carved warrior from a ninth-century wooden sled

Masters of wood

In addition to making everything from small figures to furniture, Viking carpenters decorated their work with intricate carvings, and sometimes painting, too.

Like real Viking looms, this replica stands against a wall.

Home weaving

Vikings made cloth on vertical looms. Heavy stone rings kept the up-and-down (or warp) threads straight and tight.

Leather bindings often protected the edges of a warrior's shield.

Lots of leather

Vikings used leather to make shoes, belts, and clothing. Warriors had leather shirts, leather sheaths for their knives, and leather quivers to hold their arrows.

Basketmaking
Vikings wove baskets from cane, reeds, and straw and used them for general household storage.

Special skills
- Smiths made everything from cauldrons to locks and keys.
- Carpenters knew the best wood to use for a particular object and how to cut wood to give it maximum strength.
- Both men and women spun wool or flax (linen) into yarn.

Trade and travel

The Vikings traded across Europe and as far east as Central Asia and Russia. They bought silver, silk, wine, spices, jewelry, glass, and pottery. In return, they sold honey, tin, wheat, wool, wood, iron, fur, leather, fish, and walrus ivory. Everywhere they went, the Vikings bought and sold slaves.

Northern treasure
From their own lands and from Greenland and Iceland, Vikings took furs, skins, and ivory to trading centers in western Europe.

These walrus-tusk chess pieces found on the Isle of Lewis, were probably lost on the way to being sold in England or Scotland.

Golden nuggets
Amber (fossilized tree resin) was traded widely—in its rough state, or as beads.

How much?

Small scales like these were used throughout the Viking world to weigh silver and other precious metals. Before coins were used, goods were bought with hack silver.

Set of trader's scales from Sweden.

Getting around

The Vikings navigated Russian rivers in boats they carried overland. The rivers were full of rocks and rapids that made traveling difficult, so many people died on these trips.

A piece of hack

Viking traders bought wheat in Britain.

Vikings created "hack silver" by chopping up jewelry and bars of silver. The weight was often more important to the Vikings than the way the silver looked.

Hack silver

Viking coins

This bronze Buddha was made in India in the 6th or 7th century. It was found in the Swedish trading center of Helgo.

Goods in return

Coins were in use only during the later Viking age. Before that, goods were bought with pieces of silver, or traded directly for other goods of similar value. Coins were made in large quantities under King Harald Bluetooth in 975 CE.

Who's who?

In Viking communities, there were three classes of people. At the lowest level were slaves, who were owned by other people. In the middle were freemen, and at the top were the rich nobles, who had lots of land and many servants.

Slaves

Thralls (slaves) were usually captured in other countries. Female slaves cooked, weaved, and ground grain. Male *thralls* did hard labor in th fields. Slaves could be freed by their owners or they could buy their own freedom.

Freemen at work

Freemen, also called *karls*, owned their own farms, livestock, and land. Some were also traders. This was the class that went off to war and on raids.

Vikings farmed different types of sheep. This sheep, a Manx Loghtan, sheds its own wool.

Full house

Freemen lived in basic homes. They sat on raised platforms or on stools. If there weren't enough seats, they sat on the floor. Extended families lived together in cramped conditions.

Vikings raised chickens to eat and for their eggs.

What is a Thing?

Local assemblies met at a Thing to discuss laws and sort out problems. This stream runs through the site of the Althing in Iceland, where the governing assembly met once a year. Rich nobles and freemen could all have their say at a Thing. Toward the end of the Viking age Norway, Denmark, and Sweden had their own kings so Things were no longer held.

The house of a noble man

The *jarl* class included kings and nobles who could afford large and luxurious homes. Richer Vikings had furniture such as chairs and beds; nobles even had fine tablecloths. The wealthy used imported pottery and pitchers.

The rich drank from glass, pewter, or silver cups as well as drinking horns. The poor used wooden mugs.

Nobles slept on beds similar to this replica. Rich people probably slept on mattresses made of feathers.

Rags to riches

● *Thralls* wore neck collars to show they weren't free. Female slaves had to keep their hair cut short.

● Nobles used decorated pottery, knives, and spoons.

● "Hundred" was the name for the area governed by a Thing.

Women and children

Viking women had a lot of power—they could choose their husband and divorce him if he was unfaithful or violent. The wives of freemen and chieftains could voice their opinion in legal or political debates.

Boys played with wooden toy weapons. They learned how to use real weapons in their early teens.

Replica of a painted doll

Wooden board game

No school!
Viking children didn't go to school; instead they helped at home with cooking, weaving, and spinning. They worked in fields and workshops as well.

Sewing and weaving
Viking mothers often made the clothes for their family, and almost every Viking woman spent part of her day spinning, weaving, or sewing.

Wool for spinning was collected from sheep.

This woman is braiding a woolen strap, using her toe to keep the braid in place.

Hard workers

Viking women took a lot of pride in their work. Praise was given to women for their skills at housekeeping and handiwork, such as embroidery.

In addition to making bread, women ground flour from wheat or barley.

Independent women

While men were away on expeditions, women looked after the farms and households. They were extremely capable and independent. Female slaves were often put to work as nannies.

A woman grinds grain on a quern.

Creative cooking

Women did most of the cooking in Viking homes. The food that Vikings ate depended on the season and where they lived, so women had to be creative with their recipes.

Fun and games

Vikings enjoyed themselves as much as we do. They held great feasts, where they played music, danced, and told stories. In the summer, they went swimming, fishing, and boating, and when winter came, they took to their skates, skis, and sleds.

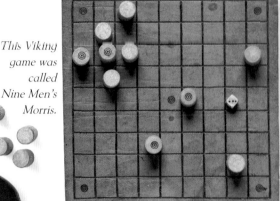

This Viking game was called Nine Men's Morris.

Danish amber gaming piece

Board games

Vikings played games scratched onto wood, stone, or leather. Pieces of bone or broken crockery were used as counters. Some boards were more elaborate, with decorative carved pieces.

Winter games

Many winter sports that Vikings engaged in were the same as today. "Ski" is a Norwegian word. People have been skiing in Norway for at least 5,000 years.

This illustration shows Ullr, the Viking god of skiing and archery.

Vikings called ice skates "ice legs." To make them they tied an animal bone to the bottom of a leather boot.

Having fun

• Ball games were also popular. Some were a bit like hockey, but they were usually played with a wooden ball.

• Vikings liked to swim and would compete to see who could stay under water for the longest time.

Silly dances

Feasts were a time for eating, drinking, and relaxing. Jugglers and jesters entertained guests with tricks and funny dances. Kings had their own poets, called skalds, who performed and praised their ruler.

Viking silver figure that may represent a dancing god.

Vikings enjoyed drinking wine, beer, and mead (a honey-based beer) at feasts.

Making music

The harp or lyre was played by musicians in rich households while stories were told. Singers performed at feasts and the audience might join in to sing a popular folk song or ballad.

Vikings loved to dance at feasts. Dances ranged from slow to fast and wild.

Harpists performed in rich Viking households.

Both men and women played music at feasts.

This Viking flute was made from a sheep's leg bone. Flutes were played like modern recorders.

This church doorway from Hylestad, Norway, was carved around the year 1200.

Storytime

The Vikings left few records in words or in pictures. In a medieval stave church in Norway, however, there is an intricate carved panel that illustrates the ancient legend of Sigurd the dragon slayer.

Sigurd's story

Perhaps the best known of all Viking legends, the tale of Sigurd appears in a wide range of early Scandinavian and Icelandic writing. It's a violent and magical saga that involves lost gold, a slain dragon, and a hero who can speak the language of birds.

This detail shows one of the characters thrown into a pit of snakes, which he tries to charm by playing a lyre with his toes.

Thrilling sagas

Skalds were Norse poets who wrote and recited stories of adventure and bravery. These spoken stories usually involved battles between good and evil, and noble warriors who conquered far-off lands and brought home treasure. Often, they married the daughters of kings, reigned over lands, and had large families.

Magical beasts

Snakes were common in Viking lands and they featured in sagas and poetry, as did mythical creatures such as dragons. This detail from a door on the Oslo City Hall in Norway shows a Viking warrior fighting a snake.

This replica casket is engraved with mythical animals.

Here, Sigurd sucks his thumb while he cooks the heart of the slain dragon.

Sharing stories

Instead of writing them down, the Vikings learned their stories by heart and passed them down from father to son. They believed that their all-powerful god Odin gave them a gift for storytelling.

Legends and beliefs

This 12th-century Swedish tapestry depicts Odin, Thor, and Frey.

Before Christianity arrived, Vikings believed in gods like Odin (father of the gods), Thor (god of thunder), and Frey (god of fertility). People made lots of figures of their gods, they worshipped them outdoors, and they passed their beliefs down from one generation to the next.

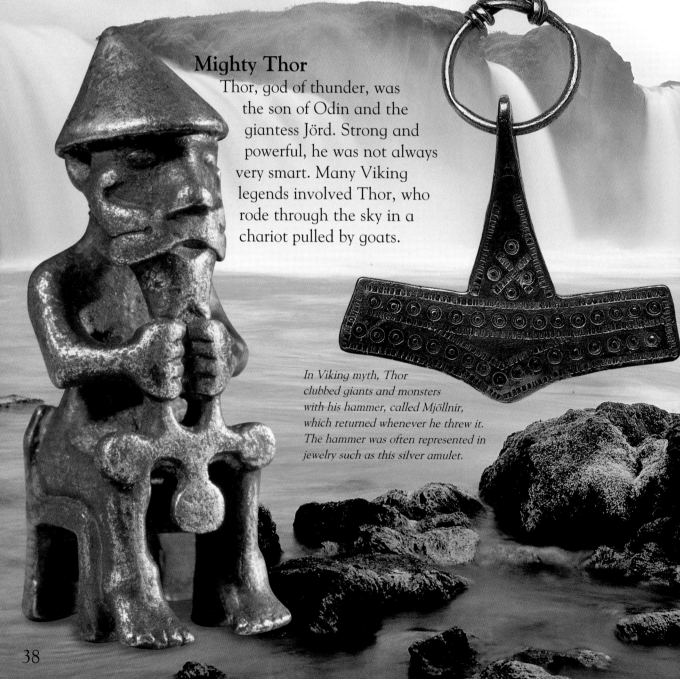

Mighty Thor

Thor, god of thunder, was the son of Odin and the giantess Jörd. Strong and powerful, he was not always very smart. Many Viking legends involved Thor, who rode through the sky in a chariot pulled by goats.

In Viking myth, Thor clubbed giants and monsters with his hammer, called Mjöllnir, which returned whenever he threw it. The hammer was often represented in jewelry such as this silver amulet.

Sacred water

Vikings worshipped at the Godafoss waterfall in Iceland (below). Its name means "waterfall of the gods."

Going to glory

Vikings called their heaven Valhalla. The engraving on this stone shows a warrior hero entering in triumph.

Loving gods

Vikings called on Frey to bless their marriages. Legends tell that his sister Freyja, goddess of love and beauty, married the mysterious god Od, who disappeared soon after. She cried for him and her tears turned to gold.

Supreme being

The great god Odin was responsible for mystery, poetry, wisdom, and war. All those who died in battle were believed to become sons of Odin.

Viking burials

Before they converted to Christianity, Vikings were buried with supplies and possessions for the afterlife—everything from clothes, cooking equipment, and furniture to animals and even servants.

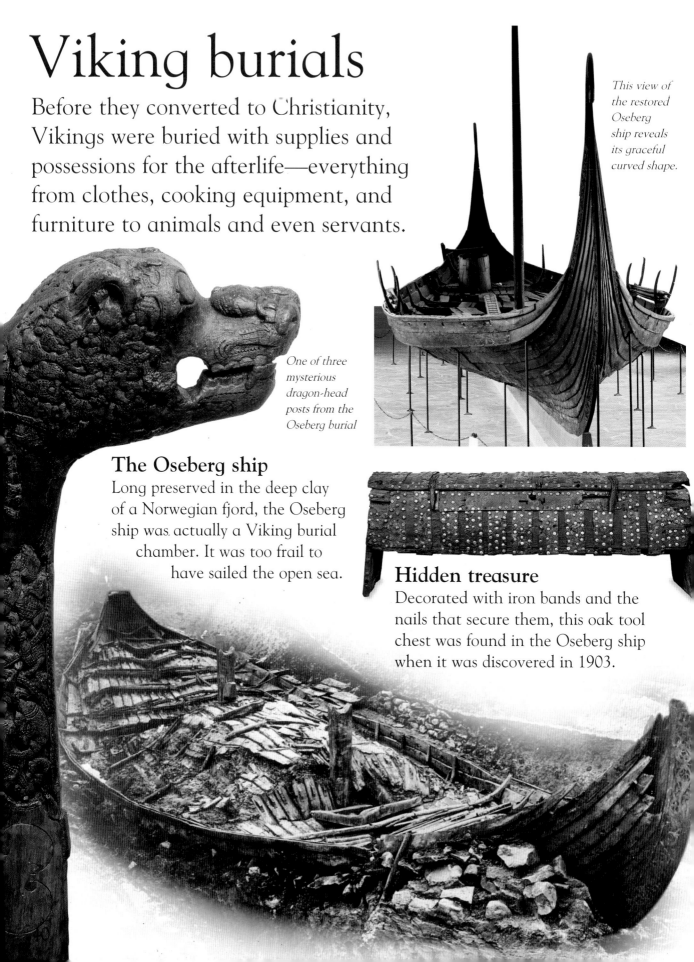

This view of the restored Oseberg ship reveals its graceful curved shape.

One of three mysterious dragon-head posts from the Oseberg burial

The Oseberg ship

Long preserved in the deep clay of a Norwegian fjord, the Oseberg ship was actually a Viking burial chamber. It was too frail to have sailed the open sea.

Hidden treasure

Decorated with iron bands and the nails that secure them, this oak tool chest was found in the Oseberg ship when it was discovered in 1903.

Bridle finery
This section of a horse's bridle was found in the grave of a rich man.

In honor
This monument at Jelling, Denmark, was built by King Harald Bluetooth as a memorial to his parents (see page 42).

Engraved silver cup found near the Jelling burial mound

Ships of stone
Poor Vikings were never buried in ships, but many decorated their grave sites with raised stones laid out in the shape of a ship.

Written in stone

Unlike other ancient cultures, the Vikings didn't write on paper, or on anything that was like paper. Almost all their pictures and records were carved in stone, or sometimes in wood. The letters in their alphabet (called runes) were straight and simple, so they could be carved easily.

Timeless shapes

Using simple tools and specialist knowledge and skill, a present-day stone cutter attempts to recreate an elaborately carved Viking monument.

Viking graffiti

This reconstruction of the Jelling stone displays one of the two sides with carved pictures: this one shows mythical beasts.

The pictures would originally have been brightly painted.

Ancient graffiti

During his travels through Greece, a Viking traveler carved runes on this stone lion in the Greek port of Piraeus.

Ribbon shapes form a border around the carved inscription.

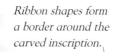

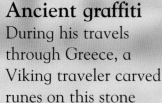

Memorial stone

Raised by King Harald Bluetooth as a monument to his parents, this great stone is at the royal burial site of Jelling in Denmark. One of the three sides of the stone is covered in runes.

Giant Torch Year Sun Thor Water

f u th a r k h n i a s t b m l r

A, b, c = f, u, th

Runes varied slightly from region to region, but the most common runic alphabet is known as *futhark* after the first three characters (*th* is one character). As well as being like letters, each of these represented a word, like 'year' or 'sun'.

Runes were thought to have magical properties. Carved onto small stones, they were used to tell the future, heal the sick, and bless people, places, and objects.

Vikings kept fine combs in cases to protect them.

Standing stones

More than 3,000 Viking rune stones have been discovered—mostly in Scandinavia, but also in the rest of Europe. This one is a monument to a Danish king who died in the 10th century.

Proud owner

In everyday life, the Vikings didn't use runes to tell stories, but for practical purposes such as labeling objects. This comb case carries the inscription, "Thorfast made a good comb." Engraved on weapons, runes were thought to enhance their power in battle.

The coming of Christianity

Viking raiders and traders came across Christian beliefs throughout Europe. It took them a while to embrace the new faith. Some were only persuaded when they saw that Christian missionaries and kings were not struck down by Viking gods.

Stave church (made from wooden planks) in the Folk Museum in Oslo, Norway

Wooden crosses decorate the portals.

Cross for protection
Viking traders often wore a cross so they could travel easily through Christian countries. This cross is from Birka in Uppland, Sweden.

The Vikings retained traces of their beliefs. The dragon heads that adorn the gables of this church are inspired by Viking mythology.

Buildings and burials
When the Vikings became Christians, they built churches all over Scandinavia. Christian Vikings also stopped burying the dead with their possessions and adopted simpler Christian burials.

Soapstone mold from
Himmerland in Denmark

Thor's
hammer

Hammers and crosses

An enterprising craftsman used one mold to make Thor's hammer and the Christian cross. Many Christian Vikings held onto a belief in Thor as a kind of religious backup.

Christian cross

Saint Ansgar

These carvings found in a church in Sweden show Saint Ansgar bringing Christianity to Scandinavia. He was invited by the Swedish king Björn to set up a church.

Early Easter eggs

This beautifully decorated egg represents Christ's resurrection from the grave. It may have been brought to the Vikings in Sweden by Russian missionaries.

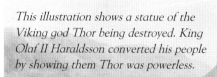

Resurrection egg
made in Russia

Crucifix carved
from oak and
gilded with copper

This illustration shows a statue of the Viking god Thor being destroyed. King Olaf II Haraldsson converted his people by showing them Thor was powerless.

Christ the King

Christ is shown as a king with a crown in this Danish representation of the crucifixion. Only Christ's hands are nailed to the cross and he looks victorious.

Kings and Christianity

In Norway, King Olaf II Haraldsson made his people adopt Christian beliefs. He saw Christianity as a way of strengthening his control of the kingdom by emphasizing the rule of law rather than the power of the sword.

Glossary

Here are the meanings of some words that are useful to know
when you're learning about Vikings.

baldric leather strap worn across the body to hold a sword.

barbarian coarse, wild, or uncultured person. Vikings were thought to be barbarians.

boss knob or stud that sticks out. Viking shields had bosses.

bow prow (or front) of a ship (opposite of **stern**).

casket small box or chest, often decorated, that holds valuables or religious relics.

cauldron large iron or stone cooking pot that Vikings hung over a fire.

chain mail flexible, protective armor made from tiny iron rings linked together almost like knitting.

daub clay or dung plastered over **wattle** to make walls or fences.

figurehead ornamental carving on the prow of a ship.

fjord long, thin, finger-shaped body of water that extends inland from an ocean or sea, often between high cliffs.

futhark a basic early Scandinavian alphabet named after its first six letters. (*see also* **rune**)

guard metal collar between the blade of a sword and its handle that protects the user's hand.

hack silver chopped-up pieces of jewelry and coins that were used as money.

hilt the handle of a sword or a dagger.

hneftafl Viking game played with wooden counters on a wooden or leather board.

hoard stash of buried Viking treasure, which could include jewelry, coins, or anything else made from precious metal.

hull body or frame of a ship.

jarl earl, noble, or chieftain; one of the three classes in Viking society. (*see also* **karl, thrall**)

karl freeman (not slave); largest of the three classes in Viking society. (*see also* **jarl, thrall**)

keel long section of wood that extends along the base of a ship from prow to stern. A ship's framework is built on its keel.

longship ship powered by lines of rowers as well as by one rectangular sail.

mast wooden or iron pole that supports a ship's sail.

missionary a person who tries to convert someone else to a different faith from the one they believe in.

New World mainly used to refer to North and South America, which were unfamiliar to ancient people.

niello black metallic compound of sulfur with silver, lead, or copper used for decoration in silver etc.

plunder to take goods by force. The Vikings plundered villages, farms, and churches wherever they traveled.

prow front section of a ship or boat (opposite of **stern**).

quern small round stone for grinding wheat into flour.

rampart mound of dirt and turf supported on a wooden framework. Ramparts were used for defense.

rigging arrangement of a ship's mast, sails, rope, etc.

runes early Scandinavian letters based on Greek and Roman characters, but simplified to make them easier to carve.

skald Viking entertainer who wrote and recited stories in poetry form about kings, battles, and heroes.

sled flat surface on runners. People traveled on sleds, but they were also used to carry heavy loads.

smith someone who works with metal, such as a goldsmith, a silversmith, or a tinsmith. Blacksmiths work with iron.

spindle small rod with tapered ends used in spinning for twisting and winding yarn.

stave upright wooden plank, post, or log used in the construction of buildings.

stern rear section of a ship (opposite of **bow** or **prow**).

sternpost ornamental carving on the stern of a ship.

Thing local assembly. All freemen could express opinions at their Thing, and the people of every district had to obey its rules.

thrall Viking slave. A slave is a person who is owned by another person, usually for the purpose of doing some kind of work; one of the three classes in Viking society. (*see also* **jarl**, **karl**)

trefoil three-lobed shape that was popular in the design of Viking jewelry, particularly brooches.

wattle woven branches used to form the framework of wattle-and-daub walls and fences. (*see also* **daub**)

Viking burial site in Sweden

Index

Acknowledgments

Dorling Kindersley would like to thank:
Dave Thirlwall at the Murton Park Viking village, York, UK; Alicia Anderson, Max Bongart, Dave Elliott, Jill Moore, Duncan Morris-Metcalf, Victoria Midda, Kay Newman, Rebbecca Pateman, Susan Rawlings, Rebecca and Sophie Scott, John and Fenn Lomax Shulver, Doreen and Peter Smith, Mick Suffolk, Andrew, Fayth, Kerri, and Wyatt Thomas, Bruce Tordoff, Paulina and Stanislaw Wdowczyk, Jane Wheatley, and Alison Wood for modelling; Andy Cooke for artwork; Iorwerth Watkins for cartography; Hedi Gutt and Siamak Tannazi for photographic assistance; and Anna and Martin Edmondson for location assistance. DK would also like to thank Fleur Star and Caroline Bingham for proofreading.

Picture credits
The publisher would like to thank the following for their kind permission to reproduce their photographs:

(Key: a-above; b-below/bottom; c-center; l-left; r-right; t-top)

Alamy Images: Daniel Bergmann 38-39 (background); Mandy Collins 12-13br; Danita Delimont 37t; Bernie Epstein 7tr; David R Frazier 23t; Les Gibbon 22cr; Leslie Garland Picture Library 43br; Mary Evans Picture Library 45bl; David Muenker 17cl; Kari Niemeläinen 15tr, 30bl, 35br; Nordic Photos 2-3; Pixonnet. com 42ca; Robert Harding Picture Library 9tc, 40tr; Stefan Sollfors 42-43t; Doug Steley 37bl; Visual Arts Library 38bl; Archeon.nl: 27; Jon Arnold: Walter Bibikow 46-47; The Bridgeman Art Library: Bibliotheque des Arts Decoratifs, Paris, France / Archives Charmet 29tr; National Museum of Scotland 28c; Danny Cambré: 32tc; Dick Clark: Dick Clark 26bc; Corbis: Stefano Bianchetti 11tr; Christophe Boisvieux 41r; Wolfgang Kaehler 16t; Charles & Josette

Lenars 32bc; Buddy Mays 28l; Ted Spiegel 8tl, 10tl, 31t; Stapleton Collection 45tr; Werner Forman 9cr, 36b, 37br, 37cra, 38t; DK Images: British Museum, London 15cra, 21cb, 21crb, 23cr, 24clb, 29cla, 29clb, 29tl, 48t; Danish National Museum 12bl, 12clb, 13tl, 17cr, 20bl, 20c, 21bl, 21tl, 24bl, 31cl, 34ca, 38cr, 41bl, 42cr, 43ca, 43clb, 45bc; Natural History Museum, London 25tc; Roskilde Viking Ships Museum, Denmark 7cla; Statens Historiska Museum, Stockholm 4tl, 20tr, 29bc, 31cr, 35bl, 35cl, 39c, 39l, 41tl, 45cl; Universitets kulturhistoriske museer/ Vikingskipshuset 7tc; Universitets Oldsaksamling, Oslo 26cl, 31bc, 36t, 40cr, 40l; Yorkshire Museum 22tl, 26cr, 34cra, 34crb; Flickr. com: Brian Butler 9br; Stefan Chivers 9cl; Michel Craipeau 7clb; Gunnar Danielson 17tr; Gisele Hannemyr 14-15br; D Prior 15tl; Hans Splinter 23bc, 26bl, 33b; Grant Way 21r; Fotevikens Museum, Sweden: 35tl; Getty Images: AFP 10-11bc; Walter Bibikow 7br; Per Breiehagen 34 (background); Sisse Brimberg 24tl; Robert Harding World Imagery 10c; Hulton Archive 40br; National Geographic / Ted Spiegel 6b; Nordic Photos 4bc; Jochem Wijnands 48 (background); Carrie Love: 5br, 15br, 16b, 17br, 17tc, 17tl, 18br, 18c, 18l, 19r, 22cb, 29bl, 30cr, 30-31, 32br, 32tr, 33c, 33tr; PBase: Jim Lanyon 35bc; Reuters: Kieran Doherty 1; Scanpix Denmark: 14c; Still Pictures: Markus Dlouhy 31bl; Thomas Haertrich 18cr, 33tl; TopFoto.co.uk: 30t; The British Library 6t; The British Museum 10tr; Firth 24-25b; Gary Waidson: 15cl, 35tr; Gary Waidson 26tl; Werner Forman Archive: 44b, 45r; British Museum London 11br, 11bl; National Museum, Copenhagen 45tl; Statens Historiska Museet, Stockholm 11br, 39br; Wikipedia, The Free Encyclopedia: Árni Magnússon Institute, Iceland 34bl; Casiopeia 41cl; York Archaeological Trust: 28cb

All other images © Dorling Kindersley
For further information see: www.dkimages.com